Discipleship According To Jesus

Joel R. Stroud

ISBN-13: 978-0-9973813-0-6

DEDICATION

To my Lord Jesus Christ, the Master Disciple Maker, who called me by his grace and enabled me to follow him, though sometimes at a distance and haltingly because of my foolishness, this booklet is gratefully dedicated.

CONTENTS

ACKNOWLEDGMENTS

I would like to thank Hank Lee, Missions Director for North Delta Association, for emphasizing the priority of discipleship and my new friend and brother, Chris McNairy, Facilitator of the Urban Fusion Network, who encouraged me to put these insights into print. I am also indebted to my wife, Sheri, and my brother, Dan Stroud, Jr., for their suggestions regarding content, and my niece, Dr. April Roberts, for proof reading the manuscript.

1

Introduction

When I came to the Lord in July of 1971, God used a wonderful Bible teacher to lead me to Christ and challenge me to be a serious student of the Scriptures. Although he taught me how to rightly divide the Word, he neglected to teach me how to cultivate my relationship with Jesus through a daily walk. So, I grew quickly in the knowledge of Christ, but not much in his grace. After several years of doing the best I could, the Lord put me under the ministry of two pastors who taught me how to follow Jesus daily and experience the abundant life of Christ. Having been on both sides of the fence, I know the difference between being a convert and being a disciple. I also believe there are myriads of Christians who long for a deeper intimacy with Jesus that is only possible through daily discipleship.

It is the observation of many today that the American church is in desperate need of revival. Most congregations in the United States are plateaued or declining, while in lands hostile to the gospel, God's work is flourishing, and a primary reason appears to be an emphasis on discipleship. The affluence we have enjoyed and the "easy believe-ism" we have preached for decades have negatively impacted every denomination. Resident membership in churches is five to ten times greater than attendance on any given Sunday. Pastors spend more time on administrative duties and caring for carnal saints than training disciples to make disciples. Ministries everywhere are being forced to reduce their budgets and change their approaches to remain relevant and viable. And while churches are floundering, focused on trying to solve their own problems, our nation is crumbling from within. Apart from a revival of Biblical proportion, there seems to be little hope.

Out of a deep sense of dissatisfaction with the status quo and a growing burden to see God bring revival to his people I offer the strong challenge God first issued to me, that is set forth for your prayerful consideration in the following pages. I do not have all the answers, but I believe one of the more important ones is a commitment to developing disciples.

My aim in this initial work is to awaken readers to the priority of Biblical discipleship, demonstrate what discipleship involves, and challenge readers to begin to follow Jesus daily. It is my prayer that all who read this booklet will experience the relationship of intimacy, joy, and victory Jesus intends for every believer.

2

A Strategic Mistake

Lest Satan should get an advantage on us...(2 Cor. 2:11)

The Bible states believers were first called Christians at Antioch in Syria.

> Acts 11:25 Then Barnabas departed for Tarsus, to seek Saul:
> Acts 11:26 And when he had found him, he Brought him to Antioch. And it came to pass, that a whole year they assembled themselves with the church, and taught many people. <u>And the disciples were called Christians first in Antioch.</u>

They did not call themselves Christians, but they were called Christians by their lost neighbors. However, the designation of choice used in the New Testament Scriptures and by early believers to describe themselves was *disciples* of Jesus. In the KJV of the New Testament God's people are called believer(s) 2 times, church(es) 112 times, Christian(s) 3 times, follower(s) 8

3

times, and servant(s) 27 times. However, they are called disciple(s) 258 times.

Why is this important? The term Christian comes from the Greek "Christianos" meaning adherent or follower of Christ. Considered by some to be originally a term of derision, it was applied to those who professed Jesus as Lord. By the end of the first century it had become the standard expression used by early church leaders and historians to refer to the followers of Jesus. However, by adopting *Christians* as our primary designation, rather than *disciples*, the church has blurred the understanding of what it means to be a Christ follower and played right into the enemy's hands. Although the term "Christian" is a worthy and honorable, it only identifies us nominally, while the expression "disciple" identifies us practically. In a day when the word "Christian" has become almost meaningless through misuse, Jesus calls us not merely to be known by his name, but to practice our faith through daily discipleship.

Our nation's religious landscape is changing, but seven out of ten Americans still identify themselves as Christians. If you were to go door to door in my neighborhood and ask, "Are you a Christian?", the vast majority would say, "Yes". Most people think that belief in God and Jesus, occasional church attendance, or trying to follow the Ten Commandments means you are a Christian. Some even think that if your parents are Christian, that makes you a Christian. Yet, many of these same people are okay with sins that have become normative in our society. Premarital sex is just part of growing up; profanity is permitted if you get mad enough; divorce is acceptable if you are incompatible; homosexuality is just about being with the one you love; abortion is a legitimate way out of an inconvenient pregnancy; gambling is just a little clean fun; and occasionally having too much to drink is okay if it is a special occasion.

However, if the same people were asked, "Are you a disciple of Jesus?", far fewer would identify themselves in this way. In fact, some would not know how to answer, being unfamiliar with the exact meaning of the word "disciple". And if you explained that being a disciple means Jesus is the master and boss of your life and you daily take up your cross and follow him, very few would use this term to describe themselves. Today, almost anyone can get away with calling himself or herself a Christian, but only those who are serious about their relationship with Jesus would call themselves disciples.

A separate but related problem is the widely accepted notion that faithful church membership is the goal for every believer. In the absence of a clear understanding and practice of discipleship, we have unwittingly lowered the expectation of what it means to be a child of God. Most church members believe that weekly attendance, tithing your income and serving in some capacity in the church organization is the sum of Christian maturity. If you come to the meetings, pay your dues, and participate in the program, that's all you need to do. We have developed a culture of church membership very similar to membership in the Lions, Kiwanis, or Rotary Club. Actually, neither Jesus nor Paul called people to church membership, but both of them called men and women to be disciples.

As a result of emphasizing the wrong thing, most churches have slowly become organizations made up of good people, doing good things for good causes. Yet, the lives of many professing Christians differ little from their lost friends. Few meet God in quiet time each day. Even fewer have a meaningful prayer life. They rarely talk about Jesus outside of their Sunday School class. Many of them do not faithfully manage their money and give sacrificially to advance God's kingdom. They often enjoy the same entertainment, have the same attitudes, and are bound in the same addictions that bind their lost friends. Paul's description of faith in the last days could easily be applied to Western Christianity at the beginning of the 21st century.

> 2 Tim. 3:1 This know also, that in the last days perilous times shall come.
> 2 Tim. 3:2 For men shall be lovers of themselves, covetous, boasters, proud, blasphemers, disobedient to parents, unthankful, unholy,
> 2 Tim. 3:3 Without natural affection, trucebreakers, false accusers, incontinent, fierce, despisers of those

who are good,
2 Tim. 3:4   Traitors, heady, highminded, lovers of pleasures more than lovers of God;
2 Tim. 3:5   <u>Having a form of godliness, but denying its power</u>: from such turn away.

Is this all it means to know Jesus?

3

Discipleship According To Jesus

If any man will come after me... (Luke 9:23)

What does it mean to be a disciple of Jesus Christ? The following discussion is not intended to be exhaustive, but it is a concise survey of what Jesus had to say about discipleship.

First, a disciple had a master.

> John 13:14 If I then, your <u>Lord and Master</u>, have washed your feet; you also ought to wash one another's feet.

The master was the authority, and his disciples submitted to his teaching.

> John 8:31 Then said Jesus to those Jews who believed on him, <u>If you continue in my word, then are you my disciples indeed;</u>

The master was also teacher, mentor, and trainer. Whether you consider John, Jesus, or Paul, their disciples were learners. Jesus daily preached to the multitudes, and then in private He taught his disciples. In order to follow Jesus they had to be disciplined in their learning and in their lifestyle.

> Mark 4:33 And with many such parables he spoke the word to them, as they were able to hear it.
> Mark 4:34 But without a parable spoke he not to them: <u>and when they were alone, he expounded all things to his disciples.</u>

Submission to his authority and knowledge of Jesus are essential aspects of a relationship with him, and you cannot have one without the other. If you do not obey Jesus, you cannot know him. If you do not know him, a relationship is impossible.

> John 14:21 <u>He who has my commandments, and keeps them,</u> he it is who loves me: and he who loves me shall be loved by my Father, <u>and I will love him, and will manifest myself to him.</u>

Is Jesus the Master, Boss, and Lord of my life? Is He my teacher; is He revealing Himself, His will, His word and His ways to me?

** If I am not doing what Jesus commands and He is not revealing Himself to me, am I His disciple?*

Second, a disciple was with his Master.

> Mark 3:13 And he goeth up into a mountain, and calleth unto him whom he would: and they came unto him.
> Mark 3:14 And he ordained twelve, <u>that they should be with him</u>…

Where the Master went, his disciples went.

> Mt. 9:18 While he spake these things unto them,

behold, there came a certain ruler, and worshipped him, saying, My daughter is even now dead: but come and lay thy hand upon her, and she shall live.
Mt. 9:19 And Jesus arose, and followed him, <u>and so did his disciples</u>.

They ate what their Master ate and slept where he slept, etc.

Mt. 8:19 And a certain scribe came, and said unto him, <u>Master, I will follow thee whithersoever thou goest</u>.
Mt. 8:20 And Jesus saith unto him, The foxes have holes, and the birds of the air have nests; but the Son of man hath not where to lay his head.

Disciples joined their Master in his activity and did what He did.

Mt. 14:19 And he commanded the multitude to sit down on the grass, and took the five loaves, and the two fishes, and looking up to heaven, he blessed, and brake, <u>and gave the loaves to *his* disciples, and the disciples to the multitude</u>.
Mt. 14:20 And they did all eat, and were filled: and they took up of the fragments that remained twelve baskets full.

During his earthly ministry, Jesus chose twelve men to accompany him always. It would have been logistically impossible for every disciple to enjoy this unique privilege, so He poured himself into the twelve and prepared them to lead and equip the others. However, since believers are now indwelt by the Spirit of God, every one of us can enjoy the unique relationship Jesus had with his disciples described in John 15.

John 15:5 I am the vine, ye *are* the branches: <u>He that abideth in me, and I in him</u>, the same bringeth forth much fruit: for without me ye can do nothing.

As the Father was in the Son and the Son was in the Father, Jesus is in us and we are in him. We work with him, not for him.

We do not operate independently, but what we see him doing, we are to do likewise, joining him in his activity.

> John 14:12 Verily, verily, I say unto you, He that believeth on me, <u>the works that I do shall he do also; and greater works than these shall he do</u>; because I go unto my Father.

So, it seems reasonable to ask,

** If I am not working where He is at work and joining him in his activity, am I really his disciple?*

Third, a disciple was as his Master.

> Mt. 10:24 The disciple is not above his master, nor the servant above his lord.
> Mt. 10:25 <u>It is enough for the disciple that he be as his master, and the servant as his lord</u>. If they have called the master of the house Beelzebub, how much more shall they call them of his household?

A disciple was afforded the same treatment as his Master. He was willing to be respected or insulted, received or rejected, blessed or persecuted as was his Master. Joseph of Arimathaea illustrated this quality. Although Jesus had just been executed and all the disciples feared similar treatment, Joseph courageously went and asked for the body of his Master.

> Mt. 27:57 When the even was come, there came a rich man of Arimathaea, named Joseph, <u>who also himself was Jesus' disciple</u>:
> Mt. 27:58 <u>He went to Pilate, and begged the body of Jesus</u>…

Are you willing to be identified with Jesus, to be known as his disciple, to be treated with the same contempt directed at him, to be marginalized or maligned? Jesus put little stock in fair weather followers, and it is appropriate to ask,

If I am unwilling to be identified with Jesus and treated as He was treated, am I his disciple?

Fourth, a disciple was sent in the name of his Master.

> Mark 3:14 And he ordained twelve, that they should be with him, and that he might send them forth to preach,
> Mark 3:15 And to have power to heal sicknesses, and to cast out devils:

As previously noted, Jesus' disciples were under the authority of their master. And because they were under his authority, they were given authority to act in his name. They were empowered to carry out his plan, program, and agenda.

> Luke 10:1 After these things the Lord appointed other seventy also, and sent them two and two before his face into every city and place, whither he himself would come.

He commanded them to heal the sick and announce the kingdom.

> Luke 10:9 And heal the sick that are therein, and say unto them, The kingdom of God is come nigh unto you.

The twelve disciples are named in Scripture while the seventy are not, but all of them were vested with the authority of Jesus to do his works and speak his word. To hear them was to hear Jesus, and to reject them was to reject Jesus.

> Luke 10:16 He that heareth you heareth me; and he that despiseth you despiseth me; and he that despiseth me despiseth him that sent me.
> Luke 10:17 And the seventy returned again with joy, saying, Lord, even the devils are subject unto us through thy name.

Now, the resurrected, ascended Lord has all power in heaven and earth. Since Pentecost his Spirit indwells every believer. He has commanded and enabled us to carry out his mission. Therefore,

** If I am not exercising his authority, empowered by his Spirit, and carrying out his mission, am I really a disciple of Jesus?*

Fifth, a disciple was like his Master.

> John 13:35 By this shall all men know that <u>ye are my disciples, if ye have love one to another</u>.

Love is the primary attribute of God and is perfectly revealed in Jesus. Not surprisingly, it is also the principal identifying trait of those who follow the Lord. However, there are eight other qualities also produced by the Holy Spirit in a disciple.

> Gal. 5:22 But the fruit of the Spirit is <u>love, joy, peace, longsuffering, gentleness, goodness, faith,</u>
> <u>Gal. 5:23 Meekness, temperance</u>: against such there is no law.

Jesus has a big family, and all the members "bear a striking resemblance to the Son of God."

> Rom. 8:29 For whom he did foreknow, he also did predestinate to be conformed to the image of his Son, that <u>he might be the firstborn among many brethren</u>.

As we daily walk with Jesus, loving, worshipping, hearing, and obeying him, a transformation occurs. Not instantaneously or entirely at the moment of conversion, but steadily, over time we are changed by the Spirit of God.

> 2 Cor. 3:18 <u>But we all</u>, with open face beholding as in a glass the glory of the Lord, <u>are changed into the same image from glory to glory</u>, even as by the Spirit of the Lord.

As Christ is formed in us we think his thoughts, desire his will and feel his emotions. His love, joy, peace, patience, gentleness, goodness, faith, meekness, and self-control are shed abroad in our hearts by the Holy Ghost. Consequently,

** If the life of Jesus is not being manifested in my mortal flesh, so that I am demonstrating his love and becoming more like him every day, am I his disciple?*

Sixth, a disciple put Jesus first.

> Luke 14:26   If any man come to me, <u>and hate not his father, and mother, and wife, and children, and brethren, and sisters</u>, yea, and his own life also, <u>he cannot be my disciple</u>.

Jesus demanded priority over everyone and everything. He took first place over one's personal expectations, sense of responsibility, and reputation.

> Luke 9:59 And he said unto another, Follow me. But he said, Lord, suffer me first to go and bury my father. Luke 9:60 Jesus said unto him, <u>Let the dead bury their dead: but go thou and preach the kingdom of God</u>.

Jesus claimed precedence over family relationships, plans, dreams, and aspirations. Even a disciple's life could not be more important than his Master.

> Luke 14:26   If any man come to me, and hate not his father, and mother, and wife, and children, and brethren, and sisters, yea, <u>and his own life also, he cannot be my disciple</u>.

Concern for security, comfort, and peace of mind had to be entrusted to God.

> Luke 9:57 And it came to pass, that, as they went in the way, a certain *man* said unto him, Lord, I will

follow thee whithersoever thou goest.
Luke 9:58   <u>And Jesus said unto him, Foxes have
holes, and birds of the air</u> *have* <u>nests; but the Son of
man hath not where to lay</u> *his* <u>head.</u>

Wealth, comfort, and position had to be subjected to the call to follow Jesus.

Mt. 19:16   And, behold, one came and said unto him,
Good Master, what good thing shall I do, that I may
have eternal life?...

Matt. 19:21   Jesus said unto him, <u>If thou wilt be
perfect, go</u> *and* <u>sell that thou hast, and give to the
poor, and thou shalt have treasure in heaven: and
come</u> *and* <u>follow me.</u>
Matt. 19:22   But when the young man heard that
saying, he went away sorrowful: <u>for he had   great
possessions.</u>

Such absolute allegiance to Christ meant that a disciple had to count the cost.

Luke 14:28   For which of you, intending to build a
tower, <u>sitteth not down first, and counteth the cost,
whether he have sufficient to finish it</u>?
Luke 14:29   Lest haply, after he hath laid the
foundation, and is not able to finish it, all that behold
it begin to mock him,

Luke 14:33   So likewise, <u>whosoever he be of you that
forsaketh not all that he hath, he cannot be my disciple.</u>

Have you drawn any lines in the sand? Have you said to God, "I will go this far and no farther."? Are you holding anything back from Jesus? That is not the mindset of a disciple. According to Jesus…

** If I value anyone or anything more than my relationship to him, I cannot be his disciple.*

Seventh, a disciple lived a life of self-denial.

Luke 9:23   And he said to them all, <u>If any man will come after me, let him deny himself</u>, and take up his cross daily, and follow me.

Repeatedly, Jesus gave the same ultimatum, but He was not describing a life of asceticism or monasticism. You cannot be salt or light if you are separated from society. Occasionally, retreat and solitude are needful, and even our Lord enjoyed times away from the thronging crowds. However, seclusion is only for the purpose of rest and refreshment, a time to refocus, reconnect and be renewed.

The call to self-denial is not a call to be coddled, but to endure hardness as a good soldier of Jesus Christ. It has to do with enduring physical deprivation, and Paul described what it could involve for a disciple.

2 Cor. 11:24   Of the Jews five times <u>received I forty stripes save one</u>.
2 Cor. 11:25 Thrice was I <u>beaten with rods</u>, once was I <u>stoned</u>, thrice I <u>suffered shipwreck</u>, a night and a day <u>I have been in the deep</u>;
2 Cor. 11:26 <u>In journeyings</u> often, <u>in perils of waters, in perils of robbers</u>, <u>in perils by my own countrymen, in perils by the heathen</u>, <u>in perils in the city</u>, <u>in perils in the wilderness</u>, <u>in perils in the sea</u>, <u>in perils among false brethren</u>;
2 Cor. 11:27 <u>In   weariness   and   painfulness,   in watchings</u> often, <u>in hunger and thirst</u>, <u>in fastings</u> often, <u>in cold and nakedness</u>.

Such devotion seems alien to western Christians because we have bought into the lie of the "me culture", illustrated by some well-worn ad slogans.

"Have it <u>your</u> way." Burger King

"<u>You deserve</u> a break today." McDonalds

"Because I'm worth it." L'Oreal

"Be all you can be." US Army

"Delta is ready when you are." Delta

"I love what you do for me." Toyota

In this age of impatience and self-indulgence many church members "get antsy" if the preacher goes past twelve o'clock on Sunday morning. We complain because the sanctuary is too cold or too hot, or the music is too loud or too soft, and all the while our brethren in the other parts of the world are being tortured, shot, crucified, and beheaded. Jesus called his followers to a life of self denial. Consequently,

If I am all about me, my, and mine, getting my needs met, doing what I want, avoiding pain or inconvenience, how can I be his disciple?

Eighth, a disciple was a cross bearer.

> Mt. 16:24 Then said Jesus unto his disciples, If any man will come after me, let him deny himself, and take up his cross, and follow me.

Jesus' disciples were under no delusion about what it meant to follow him. He made that perfectly clear by foretelling his own death at the hands of the Jewish leaders and then warning of possible implications for them.

> Luke 9:21 And he straitly charged them, and commanded them to tell no man that thing;
> Luke 9:22 Saying, The Son of man must suffer many things, and be rejected of the elders and chief priests and scribes, and be slain, and be raised the third day.
> Luke 9:23 And he said to them all, If any man will come after me, let him deny himself, and take up his cross daily, and follow me.

It was their choice to follow or not, but they knew it would not be easy. A cross signified not only self-denial, but willingly embracing shame, ridicule, rejection, and even death for Jesus' sake.

> Luke 9:26 <u>For whosoever shall be ashamed of me and of my words, of him shall the Son of man be ashamed,</u> when he shall come in his own glory, and in his Father's, and of the holy angels.

In his unique and penetrating way, A. W. Tozer defined what it meant to take up one's cross.

> "The old cross is a symbol of death. It stands for the abrupt, violent end of a human being. In Roman times, the man who took up his cross and started down the road was not coming back. He was not going out to have his life redirected; he was going out to have it ended...The cross struck cruel and hard, and when it had done its work the man was no more."

Following Jesus would likely mean the most shameful death imaginable, but the disciples knew it would be worth it in the long run. To hold on to this life with its leisure and comforts, while refusing to suffer with Jesus, would bring eternal loss. But to embrace God's calling and follow Jesus, even if it brought suffering and death, would mean eternal glory.

> Luke 9:24 For <u>whosoever will save his life shall lose it</u>; but <u>whosoever will lose his life for my sake, the same shall save it.</u>
> Luke 9:25 For what is a man advantaged, if he gain the whole world, and lose himself, or be cast away?

The cross of Jesus also represented the will of the Father, which ultimately led to Calvary. For us to take up our cross means embracing the will of God and whatever following Jesus entails- shame, rejection, even death. So,

** If I am ashamed of Jesus and his words and reject God's will for my life, am I really his disciple?*

Ninth, a disciple daily followed Jesus.

> Luke 9:23   And he said to them all, If any man will come after me, let him deny himself, <u>and take up his cross daily</u>, and follow me.

Following Jesus is not about convenience. It is not a once a week commitment or a twice a year involvement at Christmas and Easter. It is seven days a week, fifty-two weeks a year, for the rest of your life. It is daily gathering the manna and watching at Wisdom's gate. It is daily presenting your body as a living sacrifice: your hands, your feet, your eyes, your mouth, your heart for his use. It is a moment by moment fellowship with Jesus, listening for his voice, going where He goes, and doing what He does.

For the first fifteen years of my Christian life, no one taught me about a daily walk with Jesus. I read books, listened to tapes, attended Bible studies and church, but I did not have a daily quiet time. My prayer life was weak, reserved mostly for crises. For the most part I was excited about my faith, but a poor witness. I grew in knowledge, but not in fellowship and intimacy with Jesus. I was saved, but I had little assurance. I knew a measure of victory, but not the abundant life Jesus came to give. My faith was an up-and-down, roller coaster experience until someone discipled me and taught me how to have a daily walk with Christ. Our Lord is not just asking for a few minutes on Sunday and Wednesday. He desires our fellowship every day, and it is reasonable to ask…

** If I do not have a daily walk with Jesus, am I his disciple?*

Tenth, a disciple continued in Jesus' word.

> John 8:31 Then said Jesus to those Jews which believed on him, <u>If ye continue in my word, then are</u>

ye my disciples indeed;
John8:32   And ye shall know the truth, and the truth
shall make you free.

Jesus brought some great news: forgiveness is a wonderful blessing, and Heaven is going to be awesome. God's love is amazing, and the gospel is really good news. However, Jesus had some hard sayings as well. Some are hard to understand like the doctrine of predestination and election. Others are hard to believe or accept, like the doctrine of Hell and eternal punishment. An example of one of Jesus' hard sayings is John 6:53.

John 6:53   Then Jesus said unto them, Verily, verily, I say unto you, Except ye eat the flesh of the Son of man, and drink his blood, ye have no life in you.

Some disciples found this saying difficult to swallow.

John 6:61   When Jesus knew in himself that his disciples murmured at it, he said unto them, Doth this offend you?

Then he added another hard word.

John 6:65   And he said, Therefore said I unto you, that no man can come unto me, except it were given unto him of my Father.

The result was tragic.

John 6:66   From that time many of his disciples went back, and walked no more with him.

Bottom line, it is not how you start, but how you continue and how you finish. Continuing in Jesus' word means you keep on hearing, believing, and obeying what He says. Most of us know people who started out with a bang, but when the smoke cleared, they were nowhere to be found. Jesus described them for us in the Parable of the Sower.

Mt. 13:19   When any one heareth the word of the

kingdom, and understandeth it not, then cometh the wicked one, and catcheth away that which was sown in his heart. This is he which received seed by the way side.
Mt. 13:20 <u>But he that received the seed into stony places, the same is he that heareth the word, and anon with joy receiveth it;</u>
Mt. 13:21 Yet hath he not root in himself, but endureth for a while: for when tribulation or persecution ariseth because of the word, by and by he is offended.

In light of this truth, a word of caution is in order. Do not pin your hope of heaven for yourself or for someone else on a past decision that has not developed into faithful discipleship. Disciples may stumble, but they do not fall away; they keep on keeping on. That's how you know they are disciples. Therefore,

If I am not continuing in Jesus word, am I truly his disciple?

Eleventh, a disciple was a servant. Jesus commanded,

Mt. 20:25 …Ye know that the princes of the Gentiles exercise dominion over them, and they that are great exercise authority upon them.
Mt. 20:26 <u>But it shall not be so among you</u>…

Our Lord was not about getting his needs met, but meeting the needs of others.

Mt. 20:28 Even as <u>the Son of man came not to be ministered unto, but to minister</u>, and to give his life a ransom for many.

That is why He daily met the multitudes and healed every sickness and disease to the point of personal exhaustion, and He called those who followed him to serve rather than be served. On the night of his betrayal Jesus illustrated servant-hood in an unforgettable way.

John 13:2 And supper being ended, the devil having

> now put into the heart of Judas Iscariot, Simon's son,
> to betray him.
> John 13:3 Jesus knowing that the Father had given all
> things into his hands, and that he was come from God,
> and went to God;
> John 13:4 He riseth from supper, and laid aside his
> garments; and took a towel, and girded himself.
> John 13:5 After that he poureth water into a basin,
> and <u>began to wash the disciples' feet, and to wipe
> them with the towel wherewith he was girded</u>.

Remember Peter's objection and the Master's response?

> John 13:8 Peter saith unto him, Thou shalt never
> wash my feet. Jesus answered him, If I wash thee not,
> thou hast no part with me.

When Jesus had finished washing the dirty feet of his disciples, He exhorted them...

> John 13:14 If I then, your <u>Lord and Master</u>, have
> washed your feet; <u>ye also ought to wash one another's
> feet</u>.
> John 13:15 For I have given you an example, that <u>ye
> should do as I have done to you</u>.

In Biblical times, foot washing was a ministry provided by a host for his guests and performed by the least servant in the household. When a guest arrived, his feet would be dirty from walking the dusty roads, so Jesus, our Master and Lord, used a common task to teach an uncommon lesson. He girded himself with a towel and washed the disciples' feet.

Foot washing is no longer a needed service when people visit in your home, and it does not rise to the importance of Baptism or the Lord's Supper. However, though it may not be an ordinance of the Church, it still powerfully communicates the life of humble service incumbent upon a disciple. From the example of our Lord and Master, the responsibility of a disciple is clear. So,

** If I am not laying my life down in service to others, especially my brothers and sisters in Christ, am I a disciple of Jesus?*

Twelfth, a disciple produced fruit.

> John 15:2 Every branch in me that beareth not fruit he taketh away: and <u>every *branch* that beareth fruit, he purgeth it, that it may bring forth more fruit.</u>

Since Jesus is the vine, and his Father is the caretaker, fruit bearing is not optional. Jesus planned and ordained fruitfulness for his disciples. His Father cares for the vine and prunes every branch for maximum fruitfulness, removing those branches that are barren. Moreover, Jesus desires not just fruit, but *much* fruit that lasts.

> John 15:16 Ye have not chosen me, but I have chosen you, and <u>ordained you, that ye should go and bring forth fruit, and that your fruit should remain</u>: that whatsoever ye shall ask of the Father in my name, he may give it you.

All that is required of us is the most natural thing for a branch to do, viz., abide/remain in the vine. And if we remain vitally connected to Jesus, receiving life from him just as the branch receives sap from the vine, fruit will be the result.

> John 15:5 I am the vine, ye are the branches: <u>He that abideth in me, and I in him, the same bringeth forth much fruit</u>: for without me ye can do nothing.

What is the fruit spoken of here? It is the permanent change God makes in your thoughts, words, actions, attitudes, and motives as He transforms you into his likeness. It also includes the change He affects in others through you. It is the encouragement you give, the consolation you share, the devotion you foster, the souls you win, the wayward lambs you restore, etc. In short, fruit is the lasting good Jesus does in you and through you in the lives of others. Fruitfulness is the way the Father is glorified, i.e., the way people perceive what He is like. It is also the way we express our discipleship.

> John 15:8 <u>Herein is my Father glorified</u>, that ye bear much fruit; <u>so shall ye be my disciples</u>.

Since fruitfulness is ordained, failure to bear fruit is not only unlikely, but impossible for a true disciple. Therefore,

** If I am not increasing in fruitfulness, am I a disciple of Jesus?*

Finally, a disciple was committed to making disciples of all nations.

> Mt. 28:19 Go ye therefore, <u>and teach</u> all nations, baptizing them in the name of the Father, and of the Son, and of the Holy Ghost:
> Mt. 28:20 Teaching them <u>to observe</u> all things whatsoever I have commanded you: and, lo, I am with you always, even unto the end of the world. Amen.

The aim of the Great Commission is disciples not converts. The word "teach" is the Greek "matheteuo" meaning "to disciple or make disciples". Furthermore, we are charged to teach them to observe all that Jesus commanded. It is not enough to tell them what He said. We must train them "to observe", i.e. do what He commanded, further clarifying what discipleship involves. Paul took those who were converted and *taught* (matheteuo- discipled) them to follow Jesus.

> Acts 14:21 And when they had preached the gospel to that city, <u>and had taught many</u>, they returned again to Lystra, and *to* Iconium, and Antioch,
> Acts 14:22 Confirming the souls of the disciples, *and* exhorting them to continue in the faith, and that we must through much tribulation enter into the kingdom of God.

Paul explained the pattern and process of discipleship to Timothy.

> 2 Tim. 2:2   And <u>the things that thou hast heard of me</u> among many witnesses, the same <u>commit thou to faithful men</u>, who shall be able <u>to teach others also</u>.

Paul's instructions are still what is needed if we are to fulfill the Great Commission: Find faithful men and teach them what you have been taught. Then, have them find other faithful men and repeat the process. Our responsibility is not just to reach souls for Jesus, but to reach them and train them to reach and train others. As you can see, discipleship is not optional. Jesus made disciples, Paul made disciples, and we are commanded to make disciples. Consequently,

** If I am not committed to spreading the gospel by making disciples here and around the world, am I really Jesus' disciple?*

4

Counting The Cost

For which of you, intending to build a tower,
sitteth not down first and counteth the cost...
(Luke 14:28)

The call of Jesus is a call to discipleship. Regrettably, we have lost this emphasis in the American church. Well-meaning evangelists and pastors have focused on getting people to make decisions instead of teaching them to be disciples. Church members feel comfortable with the term *Christian*, but *disciple* is another matter. In the meantime our churches have been filled with anemic believers who have little joy, victory, or power.

Attempts to remedy the problem with new programs, methods, and approaches have met with little success because God will only bless obedience to his Word. We must do what He says, and we must do it his way, the way of discipleship. The words of a familiar hymn express it well.

"But we never can prove
The delights of his love
Until all on the altar we lay;

For the favor He shows
And the joy He bestows
Are for them who will trust and obey."

Should we settle for little when Jesus is calling us to so much more? Why get by on the leftovers when we can feast at the banquet table? A life of intimate fellowship awaits all who deny themselves, take up their cross daily, and follow Jesus. Would you honestly evaluate your relationship to Jesus in light of the following questions?

- Am I hearing and obeying what Jesus commands?
- Am I going where He goes and doing what He does?
- Am I willing to be treated as He was treated?
- Am I exercising his authority and carrying out his mission?
- Am I becoming more like Jesus every day?
- Is Jesus number one in my life?
- Am I fulfilling my desires or doing his will regardless of the cost?
- Am I ashamed of Jesus and unwilling to choose his will for my life?
- Do I follow Jesus daily?
- Am I continuing in Jesus' Word in spite of discouragement or persecution?
- Am I a servant?
- Am I producing fruit that remains for the glory of God?
- Am I involved in making disciples of all nations?

Jesus is not looking for converts or selling "fire insurance". He is not asking us to simply pray a prayer and decide for him, but to count the cost, realizing there is a price to be paid. He is calling men and women, boys and girls to be disciples. Have you been taught how to follow Jesus? If not, find a disciple and ask him or her to disciple you. Will you hear the Master's call and begin to follow Jesus today?

ABOUT THE AUTHOR

Joel R. Stroud is a Southern Baptist pastor, living in Lyon, MS where he has served Lyon Baptist Church since August of 1989. His spiritual upbringing was in rural churches of Mississippi, Alabama, Georgia, and Florida, served by his father, Daniel W. Stroud, Sr., a bi-vocational pastor and educator. In 1975 while teaching Bible and coaching in Memphis, TN, he met and married his wife and best friend, Sheri Ricks Stroud. They have one son, Joel Seth, a worship leader/musician living in Clarksdale, MS. Pastor Stroud is a graduate of Delta State University and New Orleans Baptist Theological Seminary. Before coming to Lyon, he served for three and a half years as pastor of Silver Springs Baptist Church near Progress, MS.

Other works by the author:

Thinking His Thoughts: Renewing Your Mind Through Daily Meditation In The Psalms & Proverbs; 299 pg. book.

Rightly Related: Going Deeper In Your Relationship With Jesus; 109 pg. book.

No Greater Work: Essays On Effective Prayer; 54 pg. booklet.

It's All Good: Praying In Harmony With God's Purposes; 80 pg. book.

A Nation In Need Of Healing: Answering the age old question, "If the foundations be destroyed, what can the righteous do?" Psalm 11:3; 18 pg. booklet.

Disasters: Why? God's Perspective On Hurricanes, Earthquakes, And Other Calamities, 18 pg. booklet.

Contact the author at joelrstroud@gmail.com.

www.ingramcontent.com/pod-product-compliance
Lightning Source LLC
Chambersburg PA
CBHW061447050726
47593CB00004B/1496